HOW TO MASSAGE YOUR CAT

WRITTEN AND ILLUSTRATED BY ALICE M. BROCK

CHRONICLE BOOKS
SAN FRANCISCO

Manufactured in China

Library of Congress Cataloging-in-Publication Data:
Brock, Alice May, 1941–
How to massage your cat / by Alice M. Brock.
p. cm.
Originally published: New York: Knopf, 1985.
ISBN-13: 978-0-8118-4069-9   ISBN-10: 0-8118-4069-7
I. Cats—Humor. I. Title.
PN6231.C23B76   1992
818'.5402—dc20   91-38171
                        CIP

10 9 8 7 6 5

Chronicle Books LLC
680 Second Street
San Francisco, CA 94107

www.chroniclebooks.com

FOR JOE

ARRANGE THE CAT NICELY ON A CLEAN TOWEL

AND PRESS FIRMLY INTO PLACE

INSPECT CAT THOROUGHLY

REMOVE ALL DEBRIS AND LOOSE HAIR
WITH A MOISTENED SPONGE

PINCH LIPS SHUT AND THRUST FINGERS UNDER RIBCAGE. AN AUDIBLE INTAKE OF BREATH WILL SIGNAL PROPER RESPIRATION HAS BEGUN

SET CAT UPRIGHT IN ITS NORMAL
SEATED POSITION

PLACE THUMBS BEHIND EARS AND
LOCK FINGERS SECURELY UNDER CHIN

RAISE CAT 8 TO 9 INCHES ABOVE TABLE
AND SHAKE ENERGETICALLY

THE CAT SHOULD FEEL COMPLETELY LOOSENED

ALLOW CAT TO REST A MOMENT

APPROACH CAT QUIETLY WITH

PALMS UP AND OPEN

BEGIN AT THE REAR

AND WORK YOUR WAY AROUND THE CAT
USING A VIGOROUS KNEADING MOTION

BUNCHiNG iT UP

AND SPREADING IT OUT

STAND SQUARELY IN FRONT OF CAT
AND GRASP IT BY BOTH EARS

PRESS FIRMLY BACK TILL YOU HEAR THE CLICK

NOW DRAW FRONT LEGS OUT AT
RIGHT ANGLES TO THE BODY AND
TUG SHARPLY

ROTATE FULLY EXTENDED LIMBS
UNTIL THEY RIDE FREE IN SOCKETS

GRIP TAIL TIGHTLY AND TURN SLOWLY COUNTERCLOCKWISE

GENTLY FLIP CAT OVER ONTO ITS BACK

AND DIRECT A VOLLEY OF RAPID SLAPS
TO THE MIDRIFF

FINISH UP IMMEDIATELY WITH A
BRISK BODY RUB

AT THIS POINT YOUR CAT SHOULD BE
ENTIRELY RELAXED

COVER THE FACE BRIEFLY WITH A
TEA TOWEL TO PROLONG CALM

A WELL MASSAGED CAT MAY REMAIN
IN THIS POSITION

FOR SOME TIME